JOHN HARBISON

LEONARD STEIN
ANAGRAMS

FOR PIANO

Commissioned by Piano Spheres
in honor of its founder,
Leonard Stein

AMP 8258
First Printing: November 2011

ISBN: 978-1-4584-1181-5

Associated Music Publishers, Inc.

DISTRIBUTED BY

HAL•LEONARD®
CORPORATION
7777 W. BLUEMOUND RD. P.O. BOX 13819 MILWAUKEE, WI 53213

L·E·O·N·A·R·D · S·T·E·I·N

Program Note

It has been a privilege, melancholic and joyful, to make these Leonard Stein Anagrams for Piano Spheres, a chance to reflect on a rich twenty-year friendship.

Leonard Stein was a direct link to Schoenberg, and to all of the performers and composers of the Second Viennese School. He was also constantly alert to everything that was happening in concert music bringing his wit, critical intelligence, passion, and high standards to bear, in his disarmingly informal style. Just his voice on the phone could make the day—when he called to celebrate his mutual birthday with Rose Mary Harbison, or just to report west-coast news, with his unique blend of enthusiasm and scepticism.

During one of his appearances at the Token Creek Festival, Leonard was delighted to discover our tradition of making anagrams from names of the summer's composers and performers. Leonard Stein (and Arnold Schoenberg) yielded nice results. When I began this piece I found, in Leonard's hand, six of them, based on his name, which he had discovered the old (pre-computer) way, repositioning the letters, crossing out each one he'd used. Naturally I've used all six of his 'finds' in the piece. At last four interesting ones didn't go in, held perhaps for another piece.

These short movements, which are interrelated, use no letter-to-pitch correspondences. They react to the movement titles, assembling fleeting images of Leonard, present and absent.

—John Harbison

duration ca. 15 minutes

LEONARD STEIN ANAGRAMS

I. I'd learn tones

John Harbison

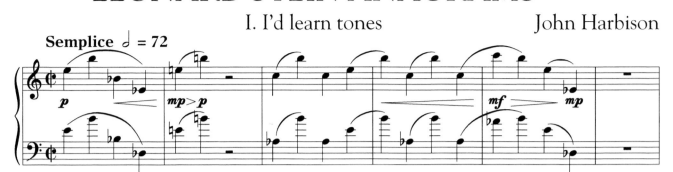

II. Note slid near

III. End tonal rise

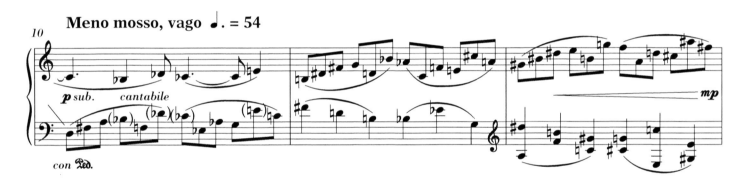

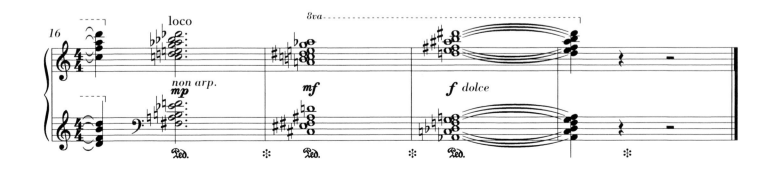

IV. Liar, send tone!

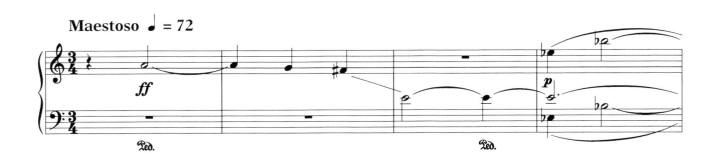

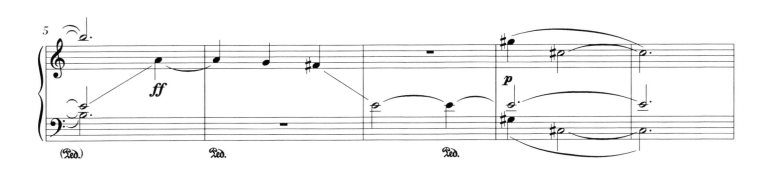

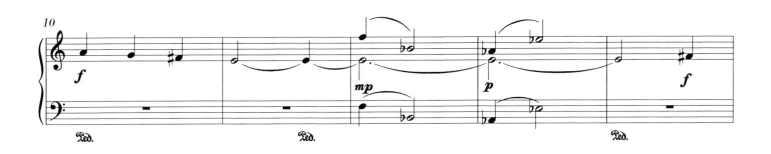

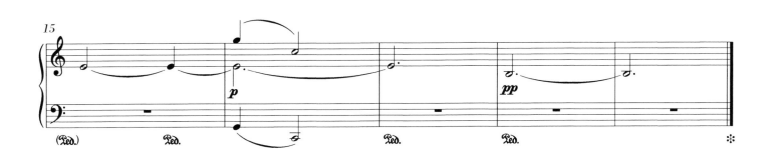

V. Listen, a drone (A silent drone)

VI. Learns to dine

VII. L A trend: noise

Tumultuoso ♩. = 132

VIII. Rinse tone, lad!

IX. Linen ear–dots

X. Tender as lion

XI. Rest: no denial

XII. Earns toil-end

XIIA. Done: entrails